THE WOMAN WHO ALWAYS LOVED PICASSO

JULIA BLACKBURN

THE WOMAN WHO ALWAYS LOVED PICASSO

illustrations by
JEFF FISHER

CARCANET

July 4 2018 and I suddenly think I could write about her in the first person. She was seventeen when she met him, he was forty six.

40,509

1. Bird

It was as if
my heart had
tumbled
down through
the blood red
cavity
of my chest,
to land
and settle
like a nesting bird
beating its wings
between my legs.

'This is love,' he said.
'Yes,' I replied,
'this is love.'

2. Hands

I was on the other side of a plate-glass door
and as I swung it open
and stepped out onto the street
he came up to me
very close.
.

He said he had seen me as a painting
now he needed to study my face
more carefully,
I must meet him the next day
he was Picasso.
The name meant nothing to me.

He took me to a bookshop
where he was in the window
on the cover of a book
written in Japanese.
I laughed.

I told him I liked
the black and red
silk tie
he wore.
He gave it to me.
I kept it safe
for the rest of my life.

3. Hair

I reminded him
of his younger sister
Maria.
She had blond hair
like his father,
although in the photos
the father's hair does not look blond,
nor does the sister's hair look blond
except in comparison
with the blackness
of his hair.

Maria died of diphtheria
when she was five
and he was ten.
It was the year in which a cure
had been found,
but for her it was too late.

At her bedside
he made a vow:
if she lived
he would abandon
what he loved best
apart from loving her
and that was the act of painting.

She did not live
and so he could go on;
her fierce ghost
sitting on his shoulder,
watching him work.

4. Pots

My mother had four children
with my father
Leon Volroff.
She was his secretary.
He was married to another woman
Who had three children.

I thought my father was a painter
but that was not true,
he was an industrialist from Sweden.
I hardly knew him.

Picasso called me his little child.
On my third visit to the studio
he removed all my clothes
and within a week
I was having sex with him.
I was young
but my body was ready.

He wanted to make love with me
whenever he was not working,
or was not with his family,
or his friends.

The apartment he found for me
was close to where he lived
with Olga, his wife,
and Pablo, his son.
I told my mother I had a job in Paris.

Picasso was very courteous to my mother;
she let him have the key
to the potting shed
in the garden
so he could make paintings of her daughter
without being disturbed.

5. Camera

In a film
made in a garden
he trots towards the camera
smiling:
a bull
who likes to feel
the dangling weight of his own balls
as they knock against
the soft velvet of his thighs.

He trots towards the camera
smiling:
a second-hand car salesman,
who can persuade you to buy
any car
just so long as he says
it must be yours.
If he is in the mood
he might agree to take
the car you already have
as part of the deal.

You will accept everything
without question.

6. Pencil

His first word as a child was *piz*
from *lapiz*
meaning pencil.
He called his cock *piz*.
'It is what I use
for my work,'
he said.

In one painting
his cock is my closed left eye
and my eyebrow
and the smiling side
of my mouth.

In that painting
I have six fingers
on each of my pale hands;
they lie limp in my lap
like the flippers
of a seal.

He told me
he could also see
with his cock.
I imagined a periscope
patrolling the ocean.

7. Horsehair

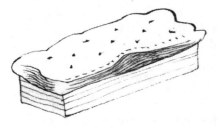

The air inside the beach hut at Dinard
smelt of beach and hut,
of sea salt, old wood,
and darkness.
He rented it for the holidays,
'I will have my siestas there,'
he said to Olga, his wife.

One morning
I dared myself
to walk past his wife and his son.
She was sheltered by a parasol,
she wore a straw hat
to frame the sweet oval of her face,
she had the sort of nose I always wanted:
small and retrousse.
She sat in a deckchair,
pale legs stretched out,
feet crossed at the ankles.
She wore shoes with a heel and a strap.
Her son who was his son too
played a solemn game
at the water's edge.
He was thin with big ears.

In the beach hut
I am quickly naked.
He is quickly naked.
There is a wooden platform
with a narrow horsehair mattress
on which we lie.
We also lie on the floor.
We crouch and twist, this way and that.
The sand is between my toes,
it coats my scalp,
clings to the sweat on my skin,
creeps into my mouth, my ears,
my cunt and arse.

He told me that when he enters the studio
he leaves his self by the door
just as a Mussulman
leaves his slippers
as he enters a mosque.
As he enters me
he cries out,
and his self vanishes;
I think it must sit on a chair
next to his wife,
the two of them waiting for his return.

He opens the door to the beach hut
and walks out quickly,
closing the door behind him.
I lie in the dark.
I do not have his ability
to start and stop things.

The days of this holiday pass one by one.
Part of my skin is walnut brown
the rest is milk white.
My hair is as yellow as sunlight.
I shine
in the darkness.

8. Water

I was a good swimmer
while he
could not swim at all.

I once saw him
standing in the sea
shoulder deep,
walking forward,
his arms doing a slow crawl,
his face concentrated
and private.

9. Ball, box

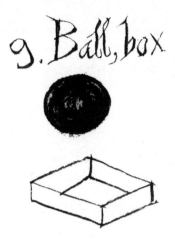

I was on holiday
by the sea
with my elder sister,
the nice one.
She took photographs
of me
for him.

I lay on rocks
that were sharp,
they cut into my skin.
I lay on the hot sand,
and it burnt me.
I sent him the pictures,
small in their envelope.

I was on holiday
by the sea
with him.
He photographed me
holding a beach ball,
black swimsuit,
face in profile.

Later he could transform
all this
into paintings,
when I was not with him,
which was often.

He also sent me photographs:
himself as a young man
in a suit,
himself sitting in an armchair
in a suit,
himself, just his face,
staring at me.

I thanked him.
I put the photographs in the box
with the letters
in which he missed me
and the drawings
in which he remembered me.

10. Sleep

I always slept easily
after sex.
While I slept
he took possession of my face,
my hair, my hands, my nakedness
and when I woke up
from the dream of being watched
he showed me what he had seen.

11. Cigarette

I never went to his home
where he received so many guests:
a smile,
a cigarette,
a hand gesture,
the black eyes,
a matador's silk sash
tied around his middle.

His wife wore clothes
made by Coco Chanel,
the butler served drinks and bowed,
the maid took the coats and hats,
the fur muffs, the ebony canes.
I suppose she was young
and pretty.

I was a secret
taken like contraband
to the upstairs studio:
a shipwreck of paint and paintings,
dust and rubbish and confusion,
where no one could disturb him
without an appointment.

I was also taken to
the locked beach hut at Dinard,
and the locked potting shed
in my mother's garden.

I did meet some of his friends
if I was there
when they came to see him
at the farm called Boisgeloup,
or if I was with him in a cafe,
but I remained a secret.

In Paris
he rented an apartment for me
with flowery wallpaper
a red armchair
and not much to do.

Later
he gave me the house
in the south of France
which was where
later still
I took my own life.

12. River

He liked to tell me the story
of the Minotaur.
He was the Minotaur
I was the maiden
given to the Minotaur

The Minotaur carries
his shaggy head
upon his human shoulders,
sharp horns sprout
from the bone of his skull.

When he is gentle
he and the maiden
sit together
side by side
naked and comfortable.
The scent of their pleasure
envelops them like mist
rising from a slow river.

When he is fierce
the whites of his eyes
cloud red,
his hot breath stinks.
The maiden is swept along
by the storm of his body,
even more frightened for him
than she is for herself.

13. Candle

He made an etching:
the Minotaur
is pierced by a spear
and the maiden watches him die
in his own blood.

He made an etching:
the Minotaur
has put all his worldly goods
into a cart
harnessed to a mare
and her two foals;
but he has disembowelled them
with his horns
so they cannot not take him
wherever it is
he wants to go.

He made an etching:
the maiden
helps the Minotaur
to escape from the Labyrinth.
She holds a candle,
the yellow flame
leads him through
the darkness.

I hung that one on the wall;
hid the others.

14. Sofa

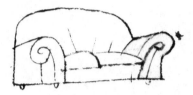

At the moment of fulfilment
he would bark
like a dog,
or like a man falling down a well,
or perhaps like the Minotaur,
who must have made a lot of noise
trapped within the turning corridors
of the labyrinth.

I imagined the labyrinth as a series of dark tunnels,
but Picasso said
it was a palace with sofas and tables,
paintings on the walls
and no way out.

He was interested
in how two people become each other
during sex;
the man becoming the woman
he is making love to,
experiencing what she feels
alongside his own experience.

15. Bodies

My pleasure was different to his:
each time again
I felt my body break
into bright fragments
hurling themselves
towards the sky
where they became
– or so it seemed to me –
a constellation of stars.

I never told him this.
The recollection
remained my own,
intact
undiminished by the long road
of his absence.

16. Solitary

The people he knew,
those who saw me briefly
but hardly spoke to me,
said I was aloof,
I behaved according to my own inclinations,
changing my mind
or my manner of living
in an inconsequential way.
I am not sure what they meant by this.

They also said
I had a voluptuous body,
fleshy thighs
and what they called
a robust coarseness.

They did not like me
any more than I liked them.

17. Dance

I might have wanted to marry him
if he had not already been married,
or to live with him
if I had thought it was a good idea,
but then I would have needed to spend time
with his friends:
all those writers and artists,
gallery owners and dancers,
musicians and hangers-on;
welcoming them
and their chatter,
smiling at their jokes,
trying to answer their questions
sensibly.

I sometimes wrote
a list of their names,
and that was a sort of freedom
which made me feel better,
more myself.

18. List

I also made lists
of his women.
Fernande wrote a book about him
and grew old.
Eva died
at the same time as Frieka the spaniel
became ill and had to be shot.
Picasso cried when he told me about the dog.

Then there was that Japanese woman
whose name I forget
and Lou Lou and Gaby,
Irene and Celestine
and all the others,
not counting the prostitutes
who did not have names
in his memory of them.

Olga refused to have sex with him
until they were married.
On her wedding day in 1918
she walked with a stick.
He met me in 1927

19. Watch

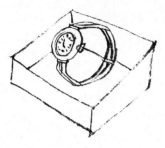

He gave me a wristwatch.
and made a painting of me
wearing the wristwatch.
I thought of it as my wedding ring.

I wore it for years
until I stopped winding it
and put it
safe and silent in the box
that held the letters
and the drawings.
It must have been something
to do with eternity
and death.

20. Dog

As a child
I had a friend
who had a dog:
a greyhound as fast as the wind.
He was not a hunter
but he enjoyed the chase.
He used to run after rabbits
but they never had his speed:
he leapt over them
and waited for them to get ahead
so he could continue with the pursuit.

Picasso
overtook everyone
with such ease.
I thought how lonely it must have been,
even if he made a drawing in the dark
the drawing was beautiful.

21. Illness

In 1932 I fell ill
from swimming in a dirty river,
spirochetosis:
clumps of my yellow hair fell out,
I grew thin.

The hair returned
but not as thick and bright as before.
My body regained its softness
but was never as butter soft
as it had been.

While I was ill
he made drawings and paintings
of a woman drowning,
of a woman saved from drowning,
of a man holding the exhausted body
of a woman,
who might be dead,
or might yet live.

22. Picture

I never went
to the big exhibition
in 1932,
but Olga must have been there
on the opening night,
confronted by
a portrait of herself
holding a pretty fan
and wearing a black dress;
her son
as a harlequin;
her husband
in a dark coat;
the blue woman
in a negligee
with small sharp breasts
and a sharp face;
the Cubist still-lives:
a piece of fruit,
a guitar,
a mandolin.

And me
in bursts of colour,
my hair yellow,
my breasts spinning
in the sky of my body,
my skin pink and lilac
and a bright, bright white.

She saw me
in the red armchair,
sleeping in a dream of satisfaction.

She saw me
in my nakedness
by the sea,
triumphant
and alone.

She must have wondered
about my name,
my age,
the sound of my voice.

Three years later
When she was told I was pregnant,
Her rage was terrible.

23. Maya Maar

I always thought
the birth of my child
his child
our Maya
would be as easy as sex.

I had looked forward
to the sensation
of a little body
slipping from me
gasping and spluttering
into the air.

It was not like that,
Maya struggled to remain
between my womb and the world,
or perhaps it was me
who struggled to keep her.

In caring for her
I lost my closeness
with him.
There were changes
to my body
and my mind,
there was the war in Spain
and there was Dora Maar
who arrived one day at the studio,
carrying her camera.

24. Silence

Had I lived in another time
to the time in which I lived
I might have wanted to talk
about all this,
to find out why
I could not stop
loving him.

I might have spoken of
my absent father,
my careless mother,
the jealous sister,
how young I was
and of the shock
that ricocheted
through my body
when I became his lover.

Perhaps then
I could have separated
myself from him,
hated him even
for what he had done
and not done.

But I lived in the time I was born into
and I kept silent,
acquiescing
to everything.

25. Hunger

When our little Maya was one year old
we went to Juan les Pins
for six weeks.
I had never spent so much time with him.
We played games,
I swam.

In a letter to a friend
he said,
'I am giving up painting
engraving
and poetry,
so that I can dedicate myself
to singing.'

26. Clothes

After Maya's birth.
I no longer looked
like the woman
I was before.
My shyness had gone,
replaced by something else.
My body had no energy
beneath the clothes
that covered it.

In one photograph
my hair is hidden
under a scarf
tied tight and prim
as if I am about to clean
the dust from a house
that is not my own.

I stand beside him
and smile vaguely
at the camera's eye.
I remind myself
of his sister,
the one who died
when she was still so young.

27. Maya

With her first words
our little daughter
called herself Maya,
and we did too
because of her authority,
even then.

She had my body,
my yellow hair,
her father's face.
I think in her
he could see himself
as a beautiful woman.

When she was a teenager
they posed side by side
in profile,
showing the shared slant
of the nose
curl of the mouth
gaze of the dark eyes,
the same determination.

28. Distance

My daughter
was like a mother to me:
she worked hard
while I drifted
within the labyrinth
of my dreams.

From the age of fifteen
she managed the income
I received from Picasso,
she advised me on practical matters
or dealt with them
without saying anything
that might upset me.

Once she was sufficiently grown
she left home,
took a job,
found a husband,
had children of her own,
remained kind,
kept a safe distance
from me
and from her father.

29. Desire

Did he care for me,
the person who I was
then
with him?
Or did he only care
for the art
that took its shape
from me?

He made so many paintings
of our time together;
I wonder
if they are
in part
my achievement
as well as his.

30.Fruit

When his desire had gone
Maya
remained:
the fruit of that desire.

As far as I could tell
he loved her for herself
and caused her no harm.
I am not sure if I was jealous,
or proud.

31. Line

He wrote me a letter,
'Who knows,' he said,
'one day when you are old
and wishing to be yourself
as a young girl again,
I might invite you to my studio
in Paris.
I'll show you the paintings I am working on,
I'll explain them to you,
I'll explain everything I know about the world
to you
and you'll explain everything you know about the world
to me.
I'll never forget what you tell me,
you'll never forget what I tell you,
not for many, many years.

But until that moment of meeting
we must be patient,
you and I,
it is not so easy to inhabit
the territory of the past.'

32. Washing

Seeing him yesterday
in a newspaper photograph,
I remembered him
back at the beginning;
sweat and seed
and the wet slip of our bodies.

Daylight
through thin curtains;
clambering from bed
I saw the sheets red
from menstrual blood
as if I had lost
a thousand virginities.

I plunged them in cold water,
watched dark rivulets
flowing out
from white linen,
felt no fear
for the future.

33. Bird

In later life
he was more afraid
than ever
of death.

If one of his caged birds died
it was quickly removed
and replaced
without a word
so as to protect him
from the reality
of loss.

I cannot believe
he did not know
this was being done.

34. ██ Paintings

If I exist
in his mind
and the person who I am
is held and mirrored and fed
in his mind,
then what becomes of me
when he dies?

I live alone,
never see him,
but if suddenly
he were to be gone
I think his absence
would kill me.

35. Path

Picasso made love to so many women,
absorbed by the intimacy
of their smiles,
their tears and rages,
the softness of their thighs,
the anguish of their hands.

But always the day drew closer
on which he must meet
Madam Death,
the only one
he could never abandon.

I see her pale body
under a garment as thin as gossamer,
I see her smile
as she kisses his lips.
'Come, sweetheart,' she says,
'we are made for each other.'

He will go with her
without turning his head
to look back
at any of us.

36. Telephone

We spoke on the telephone
the week before his death.
He sounded frail
but tender.

He called me *nina*,
child,
just as he always had
and I felt myself
to be complete
within the containment
of his voice
just as I always had -
the little daughter
of his eye.

37. Bleach

We had named Maya
after his sister,
the one he had loved so much;
maybe that helped to keep her safe.

His other children
and the children of his children,
all struggled
with an inheritance of rage.

Pablito was the son of Paulo
who was the son of Olga
who Picasso had learned to hate.

Pablito wanted to know his grandfather.
but this was not allowed
because of his father,
the son of his grandmother.

Pablito wanted to go to the funeral,
but this was not allowed
because of Jacqueline,
the wife of his grandfather.

On the following day
Pablito drank bleach.
He was in hospital for three months.
I tried to sell some drawings
to help with the cost of treatment
but by then it was too late.

Of course I hoped
I could save the boy,
but above all else
I was thinking of Picasso
and the shock for him
when he learnt what had happened
even though he was dead
and far beyond
Such knowledge.

That was when I began to miss him
in a different way.
I began to feel I should be close by,
to protect him
from the savagery
of the future.

38. Child

He showed his love for me
in the images he made of me
when I was hardly more
than a child.

I could not then
step over
into adulthood,
for fear of losing
the sensation
of that love.

I chose to remain
at one remove
from time's progression;
growing old
within the carapace
of my innocence.

39. Castle

In the radio interview I gave
three years after his death
at the age of ninety-one,
one year before my death
at the age of sixty-five,
I said he was a monster
who needed a castle
with a different woman
locked in every room
and then I laughed
and said,
'Oh we were so happy!
That's all you need to know!'

40. Weight

In the sea I could be
a seal
a porpoise
a smiling dolphin
a shoal of darting
silver fish:
movement without effort,
body without weight.

And yet,
when the time came
for my time to end,
I did not swim
resolute and languorous
towards a distant horizon,
but chose instead
to drop like a stone,
suspended
in the element
of air.

41. Bird

It was as if
my heart had
jumped
out from
the blood red
cavity
of my chest,
beating its wings
like a caged bird
released
into the sky.

'This is love,' I said.
'Yes,' he replied,
'this is love.'

42. Last Words

```
  1885
  7089
  1228
  6112
 18095
  3181
   100 (4000)
  2800
     8
 243 11
 ─────
 40,509
```

Picasso left no will because he said a will brought nothing but bad luck, by which he meant the death he wanted to avoid for as long as he could.

Six years after his funeral and two years after the funeral of Marie-Therese, the lawyers, the executors, the inheritors and the art dealers produced an inventory of the work in his private possession, or in the possession of his wives and mistresses and the children and grandchildren of his wives and mistresses:

there were one thousand eight hundred and eighty-five
paintings; seven thousand and eighty-nine
drawings; one thousand two hundred and twenty-eight
sculptures; six thousand one hundred
and twelve lithographs; eighteen thousand and ninety-
five engravings; three thousand one hundred
and eighty-one prints; one hundred books, containing
four thousand drawings and sketches;
two thousand eight hundred ceramic pieces; eight
carpets and eleven tapestries.

His personal collection included over fifty images of his
young lover Marie-Therese.

NOTE

The story of Marie-There's life is based on published biographical material, but her thoughts and memories are my own invention. There is no evidence that Picasso called his cock <u>piz</u> from the Spanish word for pencil. The letter quoted in Poem 30, was not written by Picasso and as far as I know, Marie-Therese never had a friend who owned a greyhound, as mentioned in Poem 19.

BIBLIOGRAPHY

John Richardson, *A Life of Picasso, Vol. III*
John Berger, *Success and Failure of Picasso*
Tate Modern Exhibition catalaogue, *Picasso 1932*
Olivier Widmaier Picasso, *Picasso: the real family story*
Roland Penrose, *Picasso: his life and work*

First published in Great Britain in 2019 by
Carcanet
Alliance House, 30 Cross Street
Manchester M2 7AQ
www.carcanet.co.uk

A CIP catalogue record for this book is
available from the British Library.
ISBN 978 1 78410 918 9

Book design by Andrew Latimer
Printed in Great Britain by SRP Ltd, Exeter, Devon

The publisher acknowledges financial
assistance from Arts Council England.